Haven't Got a Clue

LARRY SWARTZ & KATHY BROAD

Editorial Board
David Booth • Joan Green • Jack Booth

© 2004 Rubicon Publishing Inc.
www.rubiconpublishing.com

A Rubicon book published in association with Nelson, a division of Thomson Canada Limited

THOMSON
NELSON

1120 Birchmount Road
Scarborough, ON
M1K 5G4

All rights reserved. No part of this publication may be reproduced, stored in a database or retrieval system, distributed, or transmitted in any form or by any means, electronic, mechanical, photocopying, recording, or otherwise, without the prior written permission of Rubicon Publishing Inc.

Project Editors: Miriam Bardswich, Kim Koh
Editor: Julie Flannery
Editorial Assistant: Wafa Mohamad
Art/Creative Director: Jennifer Drew-Tremblay
Designer: Jan-John Rivera

Reprinted in 2006

Library and Archives Canada Cataloguing in Publication

Swartz, Larry
    Haven't got a clue / Larry Swartz, Kathy Broad.

(BOLDPRINT)
ISBN 13: 978-1-897096-19-2
ISBN 10: 1-897096-19-4

  1. Readers (Elementary) I. Broad, Kathy II. Title. III. Series: BOLDPRINT (Oakville, Ont.)

PE1117.S964 2004   428.6   C2004-903688-2

ACKNOWLEDGEMENTS

The publisher gratefully acknowledges permission to reprint copyrighted material in this book.

Every reasonable effort has been made to trace the owners of copyrighted material and to make due acknowledgement. Any errors or omissions drawn to our attention will be gladly rectified in future editions.

Terence Blacker: "You Have Mail," excerpt from *You've Got Ghost Mail*. © Terence Blacker. Used with permission of Caroline Sheldon Literary Agency.

Katherine Grier (text) and Pat Cupples (illustration): "Bog Bodies," from *Discover Mysteries of the Past and Present*. A Royal Ontario Museum Book in association with Kids Can Press © Royal Ontario Museum.

Donna Jackson: "The Bone Detectives," from *The Bone Detectives: How Forensic Anthropologists Solve Crimes and Uncover Mysteries of the Dead*. Reproduced by permission of Little, Brown and Company © 1996.

Stephen Leacock: "The Great Detective" © Stephen Leacock.

Adrian Mitchell: "Woman of Water," reprinted by permission of PFD on behalf of Adrian Mitchell: Adrian Mitchell Educational Health Warning! © Adrian Mitchell 1984.

Brian Patten: "The Terrible Path" from *Gargling With Jelly* © Brian Patten 1985. Reproduced by permission of the author c/o Rogers, Coleridge and White Ltd.

"Dick Tracy": Dick Tracy ® and © 2004 Tribune Media Services, Inc.

OWL Magazine: "Crime Scene Examiner for A Day," adapted from *OWL*, April 2002. Photos: D.W. Dorken. Used with permission of Bayard Canada Inc.

"Police Witness" from *Thread the Needle* (text) reprinted by permission of Harcourt Canada Ltd and (illustration) reprinted by permission of Malcolm Cullen.

CONTENTS

4 **Introduction:**
The Mystery of the Zombie Teachers

6 **Unsolved Mysteries**
Fact or fiction? Read this informational account and decide for yourself.

8 **The Mystery of the Sasquatch**
Does this creature really exist? Check out the evidence in this article.

12 **The Woman of Water**
A mysterious poem that will leave you wondering…

14 **Brainteasers**
Do brainteasers tease your brain? Take our quiz to find out.

16 **The Great Detective**
A short story that spoofs detectives and their logic.

18 **The Bone Detectives**
Can the dead talk? A factual account about how bones help to solve crimes.

22 **Bog Bodies**
A report on how a body can be preserved for 2000 years.

26 **Mystery Quiz**
Think you've got what it takes to be a mystery detective? Take our quiz and decide for yourself.

27 **Police Witness**
Would you be a good eyewitness? Test your observation skills with this puzzle.

29 **Crime Scene Examiner for a Day**
Caught red-handed! This factual account explains how your fingerprints can give you away.

32 **Dick Tracy**
Find out all about the legendary comic book detective in this article.

36 **Whodunit?**
How good are your detective skills? Read this graphic story and solve the mystery.

39 **You Have Mail**
No, it's not a computer virus. Enjoy this fictional story about a haunted computer.

46 **The Terrible Path**
A poem to send shivers up your spine!

The MYSTERY OF THE ZOMBIE TEACHERS

THIS IS FATIMA YASSIN REPORTING FOR ACTION ONE NEWS. STRANGE THINGS ARE HAPPENING AT CARTER HIGH SCHOOL. WE ARE LIVE ON LOCATION TO INVESTIGATE.

"THE TEACHERS OF CARTER HIGH HAVE MYSTERIOUSLY FALLEN INTO A TRANCE-LIKE STATE."

"THE STUDENTS HAVE LEFT THE SCHOOL UNHARMED, BUT ALL ATTEMPTS TO MOVE THE TEACHERS HAVE FAILED."

"EXPERTS HAVE NOT YET FIGURED OUT WHY TH–"

EXCUSE ME SIR, WE'RE TRYING TO FILM–

ARRWHHH

HEY! WATCH IT! OW! YOU'RE HURTING ME!

ARRWHHH!

"ARE WE STILL ON AIR!?! AWWWWW!!!"

"IS THERE ANYONE OUT THERE WHO CAN HELP US?"

SO WE GET TO FIGHT ZOMBIE TEACHERS? I HOPE MEAN OL' MS. LAVIE IS TEACHING THERE.

HOLY SMOKES! WHAT EXACTLY IS HAPPENING, MR. BENJAMIN?

PARANORMAL BUREAU OF INVESTIGATIONS HEADQUARTERS

Written and illustrated by JAN-JOHN RIVERA

WE HAVEN'T GOT A CLUE, MR. SUI. ALL INVESTIGATION ATTEMPTS BY OUR SENIOR AGENTS HAVE FAILED. I'M SENDING OUR JUNIOR AGENTS IN.
"THAT'S WHERE YOU COME IN, AGENT LARA SANTOS. USE YOUR DETECTIVE SKILLS TO SOLVE THIS CASE BEFORE THE TEACHERS BECOME MORE HOSTILE."
"YOU'LL BE TEAMED UP WITH CARTER HIGH'S TOP STUDENT, CHAD SUI. USE HIM TO AID YOUR PARANORMAL INVESTIGATION."
FO'SHO, SIR. I GOT YOUR BACK.
"PARANORMAL INVESTIGATION"? "ZOMBIE TEACHERS"? WHAT THE...! WHO ARE YOU GUYS? I THOUGHT YOU WERE JUST THE POLICE.
CHILLAX, HOMEBOY. WE GOTTA BE ON POINT WHEN WE FACE WHATEVA'S OUT THERE.
OH MAN! I'M GOING TO PEE IN MY PANTS!
WE ARE THE P.B.I - THE PARANORMAL BUREAU OF INVESTIGATIONS. RIGHT NOW WE NEED YOUR HELP. LARA WILL BRIEF YOU ABOUT OUR PAST CASES ON YOUR WAY BACK TO SCHOOL.
YOU WILL HEAR ABOUT AGENTS AND DETECTIVES.
THERE WILL BE PARANORMAL STORIES.
AND LARA WILL TEST YOU ON SOME PUZZLES.
Haven't Got a Clue
YOU'RE IN GOOD HANDS, MR. SUI. GOOD LUCK, YOU TWO!
"YES SIR!"

MYSTERY

:: Seeing is believing. I think photos help solve mysteries.

UNSOLVED MYSTERIES

warm up

Do you enjoy listening to stories of ghosts and strange happenings? Share a favourite story you have read or heard with your friends.

CROP CIRCLES

For over 30 years, there have been more than 10,000 crop circle reports from around the world. Are these strange formations made by humans? Are they left by visitors from outer space? Or are they created by spiritual groups? Researchers are still trying to find answers to these mysterious markings that have been spotted since the mid-1970s.

LOCH NESS MONSTER

Over the years, thousands of people have reported seeing a huge strange creature in Loch Ness, an extremely deep lake in Scotland. The sightings started as far back as July 1933, when a couple saw a creature with a long neck thicker than an elephant's trunk, a tiny head, a thick body, and four feet or flippers. This creature, carrying a small animal in its mouth, lurched across the road, splashed into the lake, and disappeared into the dark waters. Is there really a Loch Ness monster, as many people believe? Or is it simply a hoax to attract tourists to this part of Great Britain and keep this famous mystery alive?

GHOST BOY?

A teenager claims he is still haunted by spirits that first scared him when he was five — glowing balls of light and furniture that seemed to move by itself. The family became so frightened that they moved. And moved. And moved again. But, they claim, the spirit followed them wherever they went, even to another state.

Medical tests reveal that the teenager has no mental or physical problems to explain these strange happenings. What do you think?

WEB CONNECTIONS

Check out www.unsolved.com or other sites and learn more about crop circles. Do you think they are the work of pranksters? Share your views with the class.

wrap up

1. With a group of friends, discuss these mysteries and explain why they continue to amaze and fascinate people.

2. Imagine you are a reporter, and your assignment is to gather more information in an interview. Choose one of the mysteries, and create a list of questions to get information and evidence that will help you solve the mystery.

MYSTERY

:: I think it's just a man in a monkey suit.

The Mystery

All images-istockphoto

8

Of the Sasquatch

Are monsters real? Do you believe that strange creatures — like the famous Sasquatch monster — really exist?

Throughout North America, the Sasquatch, also known as Bigfoot, has been reported and witnessed in every US state and Canadian province. This large monster has left behind evidence of its existence. Most of this evidence cannot be faked.

In October 1967, two men went on horseback to a riverbed in northern California. They wanted to shoot a movie of the place where the Sasquatch was seen. They did not expect to come face to face with the large, dark, hair-covered body. Roger Patterson grabbed his camera from his bag and filmed the event as it happened. The animal stood up and began to walk away. Patterson chased after the animal. He was able to shoot actual evidence of a live Sasquatch. Though shaky at the beginning, the film becomes clearer and the strange animal can be clearly identified. With modern equipment, films can be easily faked but in 1967 that equipment did not exist. The Patterson film has remained a strong piece of evidence that is offered to the world.

faked: *made to look real when it's not*

warm up

What would your answer be to the writer's question: "Are monsters real?" Talk with a partner about strange creatures you have read about in books or seen on television.

CHECKPOINT

Note what Patterson did when he encountered the Sasquatch. Would you have done the same?

> **CHECKPOINT**
> Observe how the scientists look at the evidence and come to their conclusion.

Expert scientists have analyzed the film and have concluded that it is definitely NOT the trick of a man dressed up in a costume. They do not see any zipper or fastener. Muscle movement can be observed in each frame. Monster suits do not show muscle movement. Hair samples have been collected and analyzed, and are found not to come from a human. As the animal moves, his walk is totally unlike a human's. Since apes do not live in the areas where the evidence was collected, scientists believe that the creature must have been the Sasquatch.

Scientist Douglas Trupp carefully examined Patterson's film, frame by frame. He was also shown plaster casts made the day after the sightings, and was able to compare these casts to the feet shown in the film. Sasquatch footprints are a lot more common than people realize. Sightings tend to go unreported because witnesses think no one will believe them. To create fake Sasquatch footprints would take too much effort and equipment. Tracks that have been sighted show huge strides of giant feet. It would be impossible for a man to walk comfortably with a stride that is up to two metres apart.

Though scientists have published several articles stating that the footprints are real, the media is nervous about reporting these findings. Do you think science should accept this evidence to help solve the mystery of the Sasquatch?

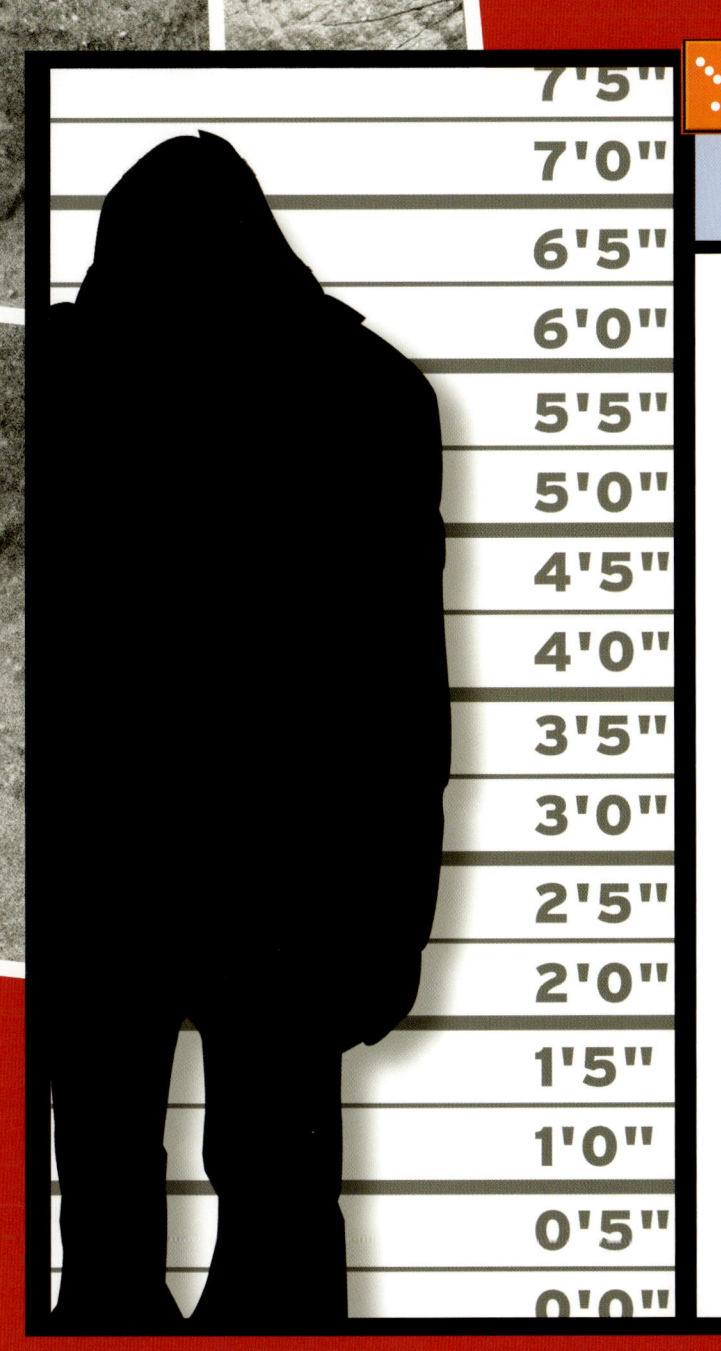

Common Beliefs about the SASQUATCH

- The Sasquatch can stand over 2.3 m (7.5 ft.).
- Its estimated weight is 300-400 kg (600-900 lb.).
- Footprints have been measured to be over 35 cm x 15-20 cm (14 in. x 6-8 in.).
- Tape recordings indicate that "vocal features would be from a larger physical size than a man."
- Food for these creatures consists primarily of vegetation, berries, nuts, and roots. Fish is a primary item, and meat will be consumed if found.
- The Sasquatch resides near rivers, lakes, or ponds. It is able to swim and its large feet serve as great flippers in deep water.
- The Sasquatch survives by hiding in the day and walking only at night. The lifespan of the Sasquatch is over 40 years.
- The Sasquatch seeks a place to die where its body will not be discovered. Once dead, the body is quickly consumed by predators and insects.
- The Sasquatch originally came from China. Remains, mostly of teeth and jawbones, exist only in China.

predators: *animals that eat other creatures*

WEB CONNECTIONS

These are frequently asked questions about the Sasquatch mystery: Where is the physical evidence? Why aren't there more photos? How many of these creatures are there? Are they dangerous? Read what others have to say on the website **www.bfro.net**, which is created by the Bigfoot Field Researchers Organization.

wrap up

1. Describe the evidence that led the scientists to conclude that what Patterson saw was not a fake. Do you agree? Share your opinion with others in the class.

2. Imagine you and two friends sighted the Sasquatch when you were on a camping trip. Role-play an interview about the experience. First prepare the questions for the interviewer and answers for the witnesses. Use information from the selection and your own knowledge to create a convincing interview for the whole class.

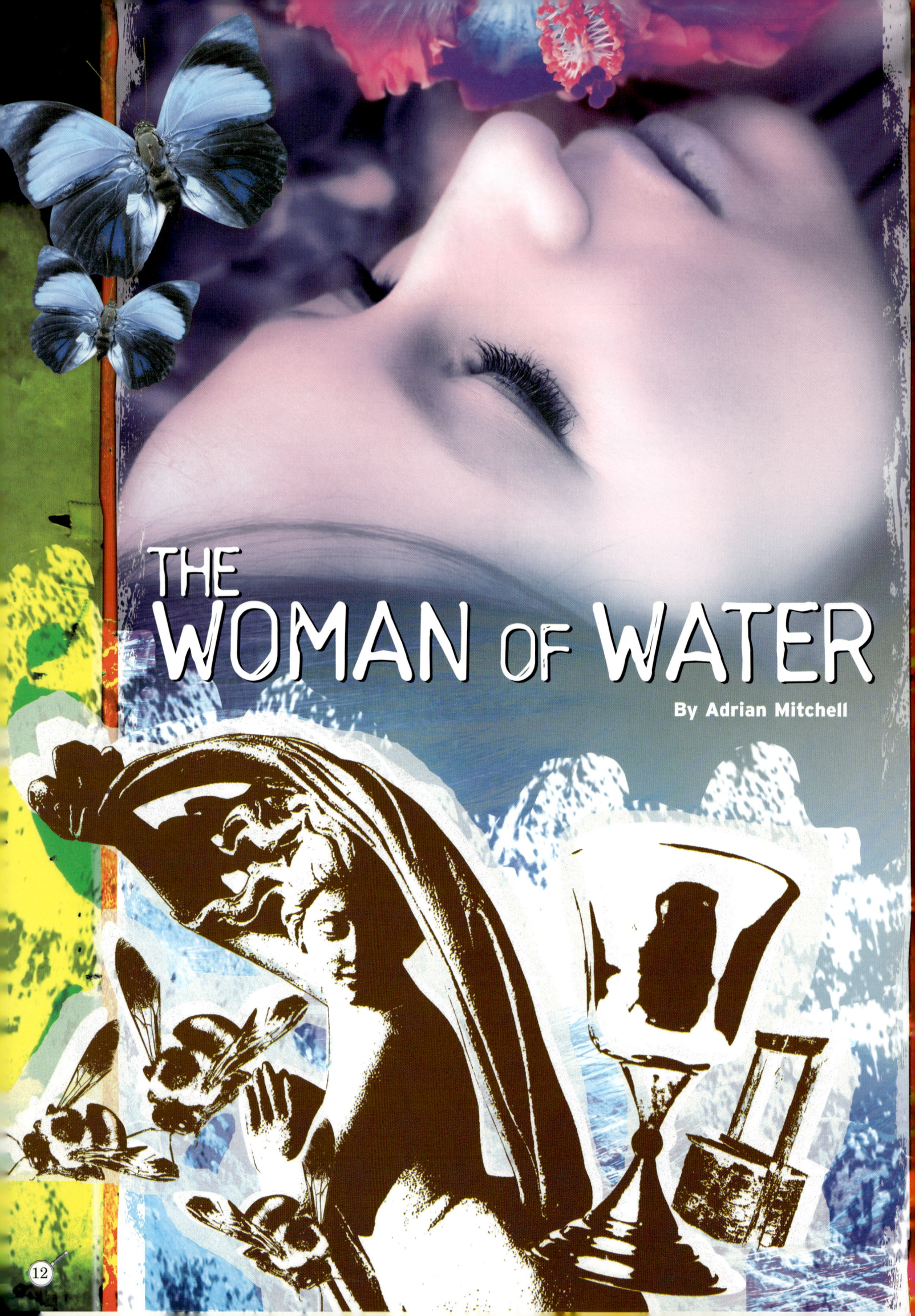

THE WOMAN OF WATER

By Adrian Mitchell

warm up

How many stories about wizards do you know? Share your favourite story with a friend.

CHECKPOINT

Who might the "woman of water" be?

There once was a woman of water
Refused a Wizard her hand.
So he took the tears of a statue
And the weight from a grain of sand
And he squeezed the sap from a comet
And the height from a Cypress tree
And he drained the dark from midnight
And he charmed the brains from a bee
And he soured the mixture with thunder
And stirred it with ice from hell
And the woman of water drank it down
And she changed into a well.

There once was a woman of water
Who was changed into a well
And the well smiled up at the Wizard
And down down down that old Wizard fell…

CHECKPOINT

Note how the poet ends the first story and begins the second one.

wrap up

1. Imagine that you are the Wizard. Create a "recipe" page to transform the Woman of Water for your wizard's book. List the ingredients and include directions to follow. You may add illustrations, signs, or symbols to your "recipe" page.

2. Consider some additional "tricks" the Wizard might use to create his magic. Prepare your own list of five tricks to change the Woman of Water into a well.

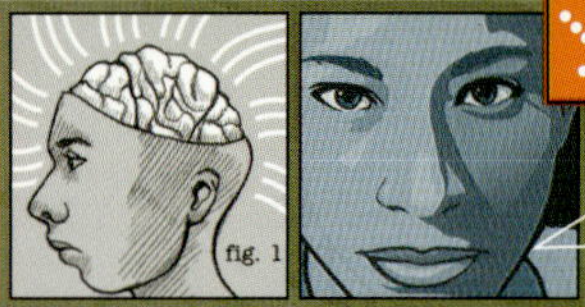

::Brain Teasers

warm up

- Have a conversation with a friend about puzzles, crosswords, and brainteasers. Do you enjoy them? What do you like best and why?

- Try solving these brainteasers without getting stumped! There are many problem-solving strategies, such as charting to solve a puzzle, using trial and error, looking for key words, watching out for misleading use of words. Which ones work for you? Do you have your own strategies?

1. Can you copy this figure on another piece of paper without retracing your path or lifting your pencil off the paper?

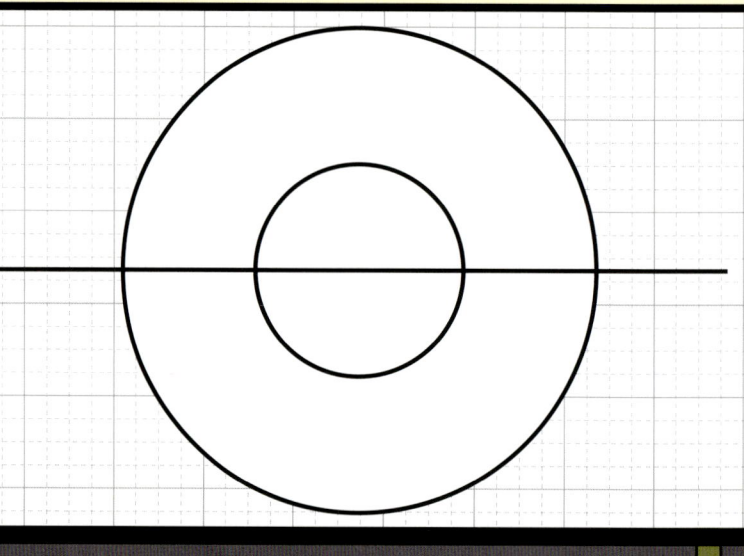

2. A train is one km long. It travels at a speed of one km per minute. How long will it take the train to go over a bridge that is one km long?

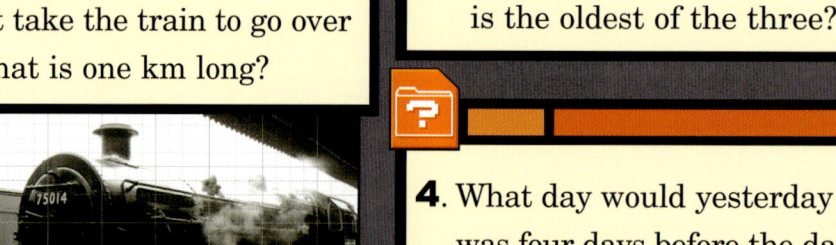

3. John is older than Jim. Jim is younger than Jack who is older than John. Who is the oldest of the three?

4. What day would yesterday be if Thursday was four days before the day after tomorrow?

5. Katie's teacher has a dish of red, orange, and yellow candies. All but four candies are red; all but four candies are orange; and all but four candies are yellow. How many candies are in the candy dish?

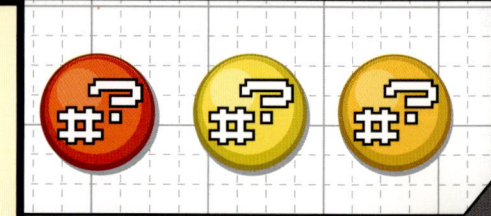

6. Three men registered at a motel. Each man paid $10 to share one large room. The manager realized that the rate for three in a room should be $25. He gave the bellboy five loonies and sent him to return the change to the three men. The bellboy was dishonest. He returned only $3 to the men, and kept two loonies for himself.

The men spent $30 originally. They got back $3, so the total they spent was $27. The bellboy kept $2. This makes a total of $29. Where was the missing dollar?

7. An American left Tucson for Phoenix on Friday. This trip took four days. He arrived on the same Friday. How did this happen?

ARIZONA
★ PHOENIX
★ TUCSON

8. A woman had two sons who were born in the same hour of the same day in the same year, but they were not twins. How could this be so?

9. A man was running home. Near home he met a masked man. He stopped. He turned around and ran back to where he started. What game was the man playing? Who is the masked man?

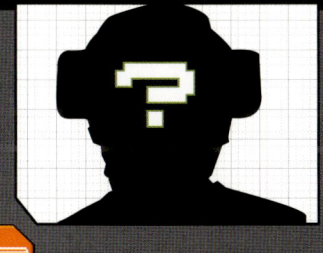

10. Molly was riding her bike near her house. She was hit by a truck. Her father raced her to the emergency room of the hospital. In the operating room, the doctor cried: "I can't operate on this child; she is my daughter!" How can this be true?

wrap up

1. The answers for each of the brainteasers in this selection have been provided for you on page 48. Did you need the answer sheet for any of these brainteasers? Does knowing the answer help you understand the problem and how to solve it?

   Explain to a friend how to solve any problem that he or she has trouble with.

2. Create a "tip sheet" of at least five strategies for solving the puzzles. Combine your tips with a partner's and together decide the top three most effective strategies.

DETECTIVE

:: This article must be about me!

THE GREAT DETECTIVE

By Stephen Leacock

warm up

What qualities would you expect a "great" detective to have? Talk to a friend and exchange ideas.

CHECKPOINT

Do you think the great detective should make this statement at this point? Why or why not?

The murder case had now reached its climax. First, the man had undoubtedly been murdered. Second, it was absolutely certain that no person had done it.

It was therefore time to call in the Great Detective. He gave one searching glance at the corpse. In a moment, he whipped out a microscope.

"Ha! Ha!" he said, as he picked a hair off the lapel of the dead man's coat. "The mystery is now solved."

climax: *high point or most intense moment*

He held up the hair.

"Listen," he said, "we have only to find the person who lost this hair and the criminal is in our hands."

The chain of logic was complete.

The detective set himself to the search.

For four days and nights he moved, unobserved, through the streets of New York scanning closely every face he passed, looking for a person who had lost a hair.

On the fifth day he discovered a man disguised as a tourist, his head enveloped in a steamer cap that reached below his ears. The man was about to go on board the ship *Gloritania*.

The detective followed him on board.

"Arrest him!" he said, and then drawing himself to his full height, he held aloft the hair.

"This is his," said the Great Detective. "It proves his guilt."

"Remove his hat," said the ship's captain sternly.

They did so.

The man was entirely bald.

"Ha!" said the Great Detective, without a moment of hesitation. "He has committed not one murder but about a million."

---

logic: *reason or judgement*

CHECKPOINT
Pick out words and expressions to show humour in the writing.

wrap up

1. Explain how the writer used the phrase "chain of logic" to poke fun at detectives and detective stories in general.

2. In a short paragraph, sum up your opinion of the Great Detective and the way he went about solving the case.

3. Imagine you are the lawyer representing your client, the man with the cap. Using information from the story, prepare questions to ask the Great Detective about the way he handled the case.

DETECTIVE

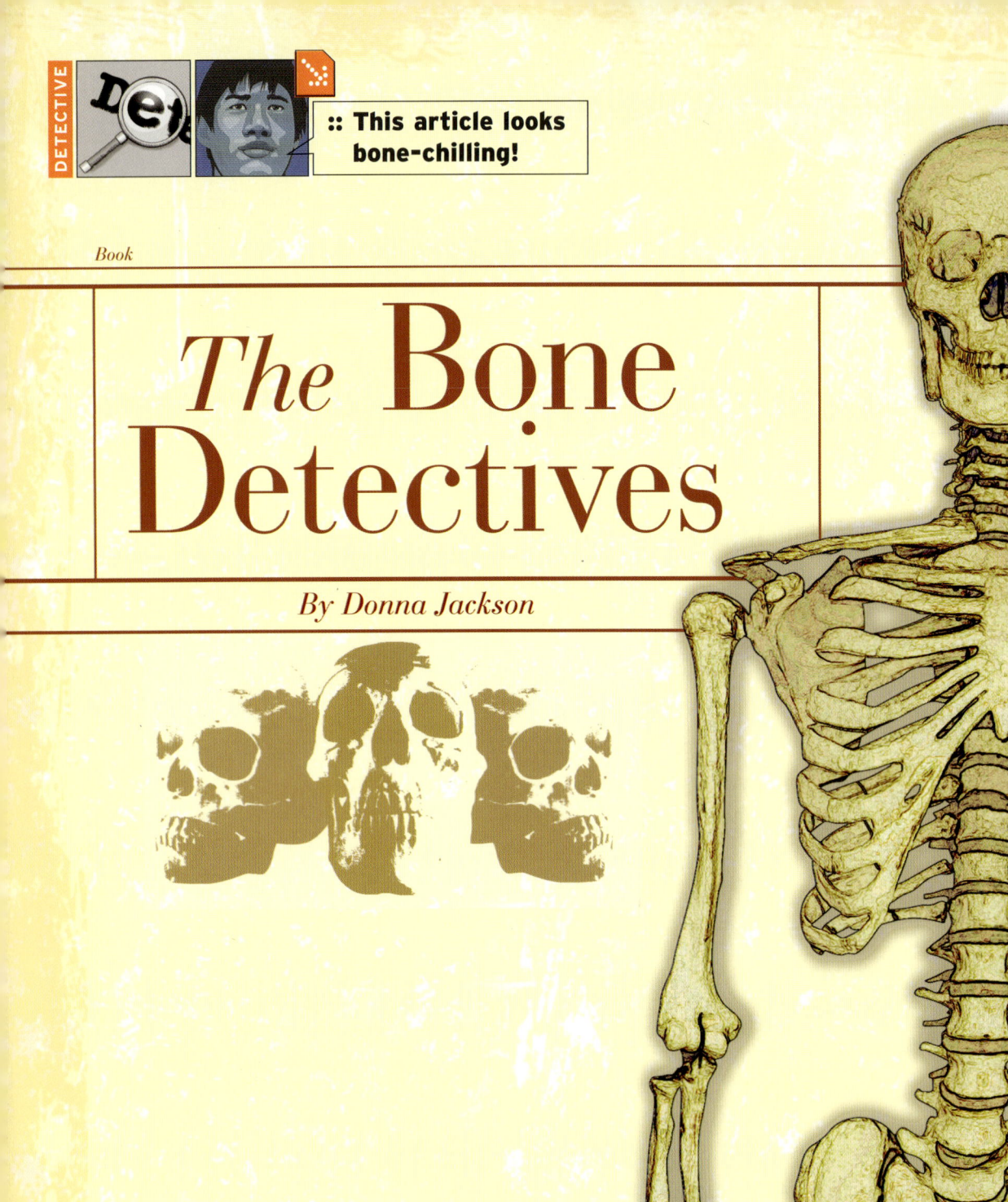

:: This article looks bone-chilling!

Book

The Bone Detectives

By Donna Jackson

warm up

- What might bone detectives do in their job?

- Do you know of any television show, movie, or book that features bone detectives? In a small group of three to four, have a discussion and share what you know.

More than two hundred bones hold our bodies together, and each one tells a story.

Some reveal our height. Some divulge our race and sex. Some even share information about foods we've eaten, limbs we've broken, and diseases we've suffered.

Not every bone tattles freely, however. Some bones say more than others.

> **Not every bone tattles freely, however. Some bones say more than others.**

But they all tell their secrets to the few who speak their language: forensic anthropologists, people whose job is to use skeletal remains to identify dead bodies. Dr. Michael Charney of the Forensic Science Laboratory at Colorado State University is a "bone detective." He uses his bone-reading skills to help police solve complex cases involving unidentified human remains.

Lining the walls of his office are the skulls and skeletons of people who have lost their lives to accidents, homicides, or time. Most of the specimens are designed to be used for teaching, but some boxes of bones remain nameless. They hold stories longing to be told, mysteries waiting to be solved. That's Dr. Charney's job.

When all that's left is a skeleton, he studies the bones for subtle clues that will help identify the dead.

"We're a rare breed," says Dr. Charney, who is one of only about 175 bone detectives practising in the United States and Canada. "We're trained to extract the most amount of information from the least amount of bone."

divulge: *reveal*

subtle: *minor, slight*

When homicide is suspected, identifying the victim often leads police to the assailant. It also allows the victim's family to grieve with finality — knowing what's become of their loved one. ...

But what if there is no body to examine? No fingerprints to lift? No bloodstains to analyze? What if all that remains is a skeleton?

What if all that remains is a skeleton?

On this day, a cardboard box marked FRAGILE arrives at Dr. Charney's office. He's expecting it. Missouri State Highway Patrol investigators had called earlier requesting his help in identifying a skull and bones found at a Boy Scout camp.

Dr. Charney opens the package and carefully unwraps the skull and each bone. After identifying the specimens as human, he lays the remains on a wide wooden table and pieces together what's left of the person's skeleton.

"I do this to see what bones I have to tell the age, race, and so on," he explains.

This time, the Sherlock Holmes of skeletons doesn't have many: a skull and about 40 small bones and fragments.

CHECKPOINT
Who is Sherlock Holmes? Why is Dr. Charney referred to as the Sherlock Holmes of skeletons?

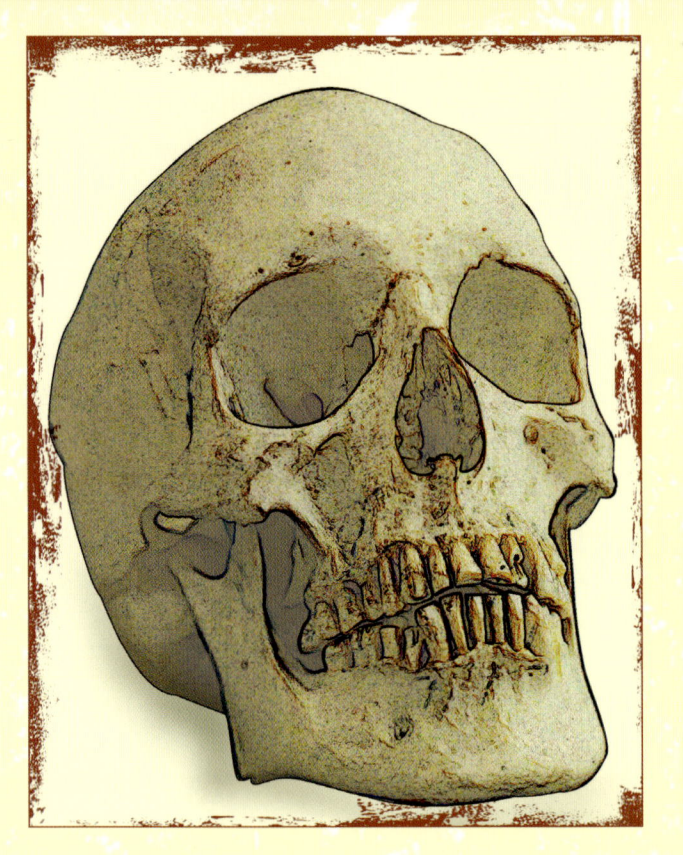

Dr. Charney picks up the skull and probes its nooks and crannies. Now he's ready to ask questions:

- Do the remains belong to a man or a woman?
- How old was the person at the time of death?
- Was he or she short, tall, or of average height?
- Are signs of violence present?
- Are there any anomalies, healed fractures, or other distinctive markers?

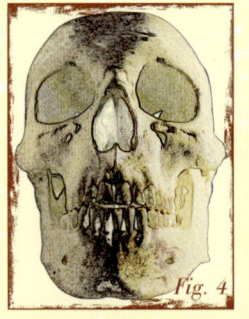

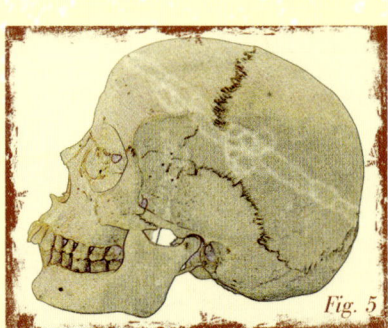

Fig. 4
Fig. 5

assailant: *attacker*
anomalies: *something unusual or inconsistent*

Only the bone detective's trained eye can discern the answers to these questions.

By inspecting the skull alone, Dr. Charney collects clues to a person's identity.

"Male skulls are generally larger and heavier than female skulls," he notes. The skull sent by Missouri police was small and lightly developed.

CHECKPOINT
Pay attention to how Dr. Charney determines that the remains belong to a woman.

Male skulls also tend to have a bony ridge above their eyes. The Missouri skull didn't. Neither did it display the relatively low, slanted forehead or smooth upper eye rim typically seen in males.

Its facial features are rounded at the forehead and sharpened around the top of the upper eye rim.

Still, how could Dr. Charney be positive these remains belong to a woman?

The best way to know for certain is by examining the pubic bones, which sit in the front of the pelvis, or hipbone. In general, a woman's pelvis is proportionally wider than a man's, making room for childbearing.

WEB CONNECTIONS
Use the Internet to learn more about bone detectives and how they solve crimes. In your own words, write a report and share it with your class.

"If the angle measures less than 90 degrees, it's a male. If it measures more than 90 degrees, it's a female."

The pubic bones reveal other things as well. For example, when a mother-to-be is in labour, the pubic bones will separate to allow additional room for the baby's head. After a woman has delivered two children, the process leaves a small indentation on the bones, Dr. Charney says.

The Missouri specimen measured 100 degrees at the subpubic angle. A *depression* was also visible on the pubic bone.

Dr. Charney's conclusion: the victim was a woman who had given birth to at least two children.

depression: hollow or dent

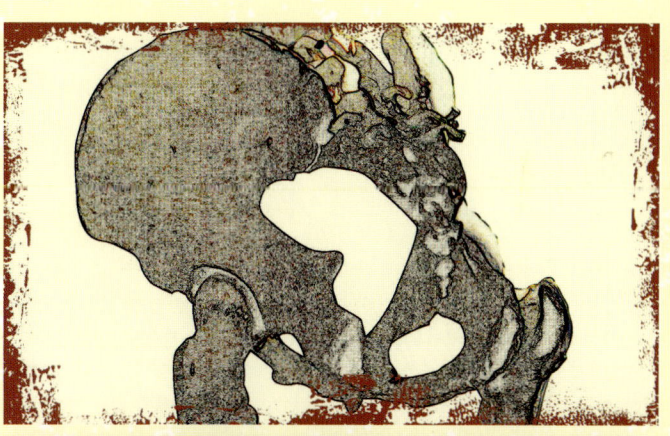

wrap up
1. List five interesting facts you learned about Dr. Charney's job. Compare your list with a partner's. What facts were common in both lists? What facts might you share with each other?

2. Using your own words, explain how Dr. Charney concluded that the skull and bones found at a Boy Scout camp belonged to a woman with at least two children.

MYSTERY

:: There's no way a body can stay that well preserved!

BOG BODIES
By: Katherine Grier

Things rot so easily that it's amazing anything has lasted at all. But a quick glance around a museum will tell you that some things have stayed good for thousands of years. They have lasted because somehow they have been protected.

You can see why in 1950 when the Danish farmers in Tollund, Denmark, discovered a body in the bog, they called the police. There was a rope around the neck. The farmers thought they'd found the victim of a recent murder. They had no idea that this was the body of a man who died more than 2000 years ago!

warm up

Do you think a story with a title like "Bog Bodies" will be fact or fiction? Discuss the question with a friend and share your views.

CHECKPOINT

How does the opening sentence prepare you to continue reading the article?

He was Tollund Man, named after the place where he was found — a bog called Tollund Fen. A bog is a very old wetland where scrubby trees and low plants grow between pools of open water. Tollund Man was well preserved because he was buried in a bog. Why? For two reasons.

First, bog water stands still. The oxygen in it was used up long ago. Without much oxygen, most bacteria can't live. And without bacteria, many things decay very slowly.

And second, although a bog doesn't have much oxygen, it does have a lot of tannic acid. That's the same acid that's in tea. This tea-like bath takes years to brew. It's made up of decaying big plants. The bog water soaked into Tollund Man and tanned him like leather. It made him a poor meal for the few insects and bacteria that lived in the bog.

> How did Tollund Man end up in the bog? Scientists know he died a violent death because he was found with a leather noose around his neck.

The bog protected Tollund Man well, right down to his fingernails and the short beard on his face. His brain and his inner organs were whole. Scientists were even able to take what was left of his last meal from his stomach and intestines. It was probably a thin porridge made from grains and seeds.

CHECKPOINT
Note the preservation of Tollund Man, as explained by the writer.

How did Tollund Man end up in the bog? Scientists know he died a violent death because he was found with a leather noose around his neck. Perhaps he was a criminal. But more likely, he was killed as a sacrifice. Two thousand years ago, many Europeans believed in a goddess of the Earth. They thought that unless they sacrificed a living person to her in the middle of the winter, spring would not come, crops would be poor, and all the people would suffer.

wrap up

1. Prepare a TRUE/FALSE quiz of 6-10 questions using facts you have learned about bog bodies from the selection. Exchange your quiz with a partner and answer each other's questions to determine how much information you each remember from the story.

2. Imagine that you lived 2 000 years ago and knew Tollund Man. In a small group, create a graphic story to trace how he came to be in the bog and how he was discovered.

WEB CONNECTIONS

Use the Internet to learn more about bog bodies. Working in small groups, focus on recent discoveries of bog bodies and share your information.

mystery quiz

:: Ok, hotshot. What's your mystery IQ?

Do you have what it takes to be a detective? Take this quiz and find out!

Answers on page 48

1. The Nancy Drew mysteries were written by…
   a. Judy Blume
   b. Drew Barrymore
   c. Nancy Greene
   d. Carolyn Keene

2. The Hardy boys in the Hardy Boys stories are…
   a. brothers
   b. friends
   c. cousins
   d. police officers

3. Who is NOT an author of detective stories?
   a. Sir Arthur Conan Doyle
   b. Eric Wilson
   c. James Bond
   d. Agatha Christie

4. Who is NOT a fictional detective?
   a. Encyclopedia Brown
   b. Nate the Great
   c. Harriet the Spy
   d. Harry Potter

5. Which of the following is a television detective?
   a. Inspector Gadget
   b. Austin Powers
   c. Frasier Crane
   d. all of the above

6. The Bermuda Triangle is…
   a. a ship that sails around Bermuda
   b. a resort in Bermuda
   c. a shape with three equal sides
   d. a mysterious place where accidents happen

7. Which pop celebrity starred in the movie Dick Tracy as "Breathless Mahoney"?
   a. Celine Dion
   b. Janet Jackson
   c. Christina Aguilera
   d. Madonna

8. A polygraph is a …
   a. type of code
   b. type of invisible ink
   c. lie detector
   d. detective's database

9. The first three words in the international call-up alphabet are…
   a. Alpha Bravo Candy
   b. Alpha Bravo Charlie
   c. Allan Billy Charlie
   d. Alpha Bingo Candy

10. Watson is Sherlock Holmes'
    a. friend
    b. dog
    c. author
    d. hometown

PUZZLES

:: I know it's higher than yours.

POLICE WITNESS

This is the scene of a crime. You were standing on the second floor balcony observing the lobby just before the lights went out and the diamond necklace was stolen. You will soon be questioned by the police about what you saw just before the robbery. Study the picture for two minutes; then turn to page 28.

POLICE WITNESS

Work with a partner. One of you is the detective; the other is the witness. The detective asks the following questions and records the witness's answers. Then switch roles.

1. On what date did this crime take place?
2. At what time did the crime take place?
3. What was the weather like outside?
4. How many people were leaving the lobby?
5. How many people were sitting on the couch against the staircase?
6. Were there any misspelled signs in the lobby?
7. Where was the next boat tour going?
8. Who else might have witnessed the crime?
9. Where was the man with the cane going?
10. How many plants were there in the lobby?
11. Did the man with the golf clubs have a striped or checkered sweater?

When you are done, turn back to the illustration of the scene and check your answers with your partner's. How well did you do as an eyewitness?

DETECTIVE

:: No criminal makes a clean sweep!

CRIME SCENE EXAMINER FOR A DAY

Adapted from *OWL* Magazine, April 2002

warm up

What are your favourite detective or crime shows? Tell a partner about a show you have seen where a small clue revealed who committed the crime.

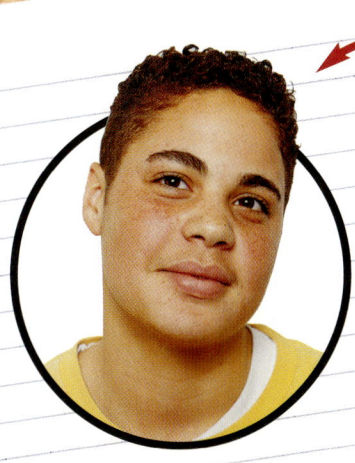

Hi, I'm Chris Provo, OWL Reporter. At the Forensic Services Unit in Toronto, Canada, I saw how tiny clues left at the scene of a crime can help police catch a criminal. Join me as I try my hand at solving crime.

Under the watchful eye of Detective Constable David Wieland, I spent a day on the job as a ...
Crime Scene Examiner

Dusting for Prints

Every time someone touches something, he or she leaves a fingerprint because fingers secrete oils and sweat. Most fingerprints are latent, which means they're invisible. When a print is left on a smooth surface like a window, detectives can pick it up by dusting. They spread a fine powder on the surface, which sticks to the fingerprint and makes it visible. Then, with a piece of clear sticky tape, they lift the print from the window and stick it onto a piece of acetate to take back to the lab. Detectives always note where a fingerprint was found and take a photo of it.

Print powder is dusted over fingerprints to make them visible.

A fingerprint brush is usually made from fibreglass, camel's hair, or squirrel's hair.

Fingerprints are one of the most important pieces of evidence in a case. That's because no two people have exactly the same pattern of ridges and swirls on their fingers. And fingerprints stay the same for a person's entire life.

Fingerprints on a car window.

You have to spin the brush to spread the print powder.

What Type are You?

Arch

An arch is the least common and looks the way you'd expect — like an arch.

DO NOT CROSS   POLICE LIN

Fingerprints are transferred to acetate with clear tape.

Measuring tape records the exact size of a print.

A magnifying glass shows fingerprints more clearly.

Matching Fingerprints

Detectives bring the lifted fingerprints back to the lab and scan them into a computer. The prints then become part of the Automated Fingerprint Identification System (AFIS), a computer network that stores and searches through millions of fingerprints collected from all over Canada and the world. If detectives bring in a whorl fingerprint, AFIS compares it to all the other whorls in its system, looking for a match. The search only takes a few seconds and then the computer presents several potential matches. A fingerprint examiner looks at each one individually. It takes a keen eye and a lot of experience to find a match.

Detective Constable Wieland says: The computer can narrow down a fingerprint search, but a real person always makes the final decision of whether the prints match or not.

Take a look at the pads of your fingers and compare them with the three main types of fingerprints:

Loop

Whorl

A **loop** can lean to the right or left and is the most common type of fingerprint. Sometimes two loops can be interlocked, one above the other.

A **whorl** has a circle at its centre.

wrap up

Get a group of your friends to put ink on their right thumb and press it onto a card with their name on it. Turn your back while one person presses his or her inked thumb onto a blank piece of paper. Can you match the print to the correct person?

DO NOT CROSS

DETECTIVE

:: That's what a *real* detective looks like.

DICK TRACY

warm up

This selection is about Dick Tracy, the legendary police detective. Share stories with your friends about Dick Tracy or other fictional detectives that you are familiar with.

CHECKPOINT
Note the writer's description of Dick Tracy. Do you think the artist has created an accurate image?

DICK TRACY AND TESS TRUEHEART

THE CHARACTER

Dick Tracy began as a newspaper strip on 4 October 1931. The character of Dick Tracy was created by Chester Gould, who wrote and drew the comic hero for over 40 years.

Dick Tracy is easily recognized by his eagle-like nose and jutting chin. He is also known for his hat and raincoat. He is a plainclothes police officer who uses clever technology to bring down hundreds of bizarre criminals. Tracy is feared and respected in the criminal criminal underworld.

THE DETECTIVE

The story of how Dick Tracy became a police officer is an interesting one. As a young man, Tracy was a commercial diver. He fell in love with a photographer named Tess Trueheart. On the day of their engagement, the couple went to her parents' house and walked right into the middle of a robbery. The crooks shot Tess's father dead and kidnapped Tess. Dick Tracy vowed to save the woman he loved and get justice done. He went to the police force to report the crime and, nine days later, he was hired as a police detective. Dick Tracy rescued his lost sweetheart, but it took them over 20 years in comic strip adventures before they finally got married.

technology: *technical know-how*

THE VILLAINS

Villains play a key role in the comic strips. Over the years, readers were thrilled by enemies such as 3-D Magee (used killer ants), Big Boy Caprice (Tracy's arch-enemy), The Blank (face destroyed by gunshot), Chameleon (disguise expert), Blowtop, Haf-n-Haf, Two-Face, Torcher, Brow, and Breathless Mahoney.

THE GADGETS

Like all good detectives, Dick Tracy's main quality was his determination. He pushed to solve cases, whatever the obstacles. He also used gadgets to help catch criminals and overcome his enemies. A two-way wrist radio became his most famous trademark; this was later replaced by a two-way television, which eventually included its own built-in computer. Sometimes Tracy wore a miniature ring camera, which he sneakily used to gather evidence. He also used phone wiretaps long before they existed in the real world, and a "voice-o-graph" to identify criminals by their voiceprints.

trademark: *something distinctive*

CHECKPOINT

Note how the information in brackets gives you a better idea of the enemies. Think of short descriptions for Blowtop, Haf-n-Haf, Two-Face, Torcher, Brow, and Breathless Mahoney.

DIFFERENT MEDIUMS

Throughout the 20th century, you would meet the character of Dick Tracy in a variety of mediums. You could read about Tracy's adventures in one of the longest running series in Big Little Books. Some titles include *Dick Tracy and the Man with No Face*, *Dick Tracy and the Phantom Ship*, and *Dick Tracy and the Hotel Murders*. In 1935, Tracy's adventures could be heard as a radio show. In 1937, the first of many movies featuring Dick Tracy was shown. Another movie about the comic book hero was made in 1990, featuring stars like Warren Beatty and Madonna. Tracy also appeared in a series of 130 animated cartoons, which saw him handing out assignments to various assistant detectives. In 1995, the US Postal Service honoured this famous comic book character by featuring him on a stamp.

wrap up

1. Imagine that you are giving a short speech about Dick Tracy. Describe the man and highlight interesting details about his life as a famous detective. Use information from this story.

2. In a small group, brainstorm ideas for a detective comic strip of your own. Things to consider: names of characters; appearance and characteristics; abilities and special strengths; weaknesses; enemies; storyline; style of writing. Work together to create the sketches and the dialogue.

WEB CONNECTIONS

You can read an original Dick Tracy comic strip at this website: http://xroads.virginia.edu/~1930s/PRINT/comic/tracy/tracy.html. Do you like Dick Tracy comic strips? Why or why not? Share your views with a friend.

Whodunit?

Illustrated by MIKE ROOTH

warm up

- What clue does the title give you about the type of story you are about to read?
- After reading the opening sentence, think of questions that you hope will be answered.

THE CORPSE OF WILLIAM BARTON WAS FOUND ON A BENCH ON SANTA CLARA BEACH.

MORNING, CHIEF. A JOGGER DISCOVERED THE BODY AT 6:00 THIS MORNING.

HIS NAME WAS BARTON. THE CORONER PLACED THE DEATH BETWEEN MIDNIGHT AND 2:00 THIS MORNING.

HAS ANYONE TOUCHED THIS GUN?

NO, WE FOUND IT LIKE THAT. HIS CLOTHES ARE CLEAN AND TIDY.

IT LOOKS LIKE A CLEAR CASE OF SUICIDE.

HAVE YOU NOTIFIED ANYONE?

WE CALLED HIS WIFE – SHE SOUNDED VERY UPSET.

SHE SAID HE HAD BEEN DEPRESSED FOR THE PAST FEW MONTHS. HIS MUSIC BUSINESS WAS FAILING.

LATER THAT MORNING:
MRS. BARTON, WERE YOU WITH YOUR HUSBAND LAST NIGHT?
YES, WE WERE AT A PARTY AT THE HOME OF MY HUSBAND'S BUSINESS PARTNER.
YOU SAID THAT YOUR HUSBAND LEFT THE PARTY TO WALK ON THE BEACH.
YES.
WHAT TIME WAS THAT?
AROUND 10:00, AFTER DINNER.
DIDN'T YOU STOP YOUR HUSBAND?
HE SAID HE NEEDED SOME AIR.
DO YOU KNOW WHO WAS THE LAST PERSON HE SPOKE TO?
HIS PARTNER, I THINK.
DIDN'T ANYBODY GO OUT LOOKING FOR HIM WHEN HE DIDN'T RETURN BY MIDNIGHT?
I THOUGHT HE HAD DECIDED TO GO HOME IN HIS OWN CAR. I STAYED ON...(SOB)
TAKE YOUR TIME, MRS. BARTON.

"WEREN'T YOU WORRIED?"

"THIS WASN'T THE FIRST TIME WILLIAM HAD WALKED OUT OF A PARTY. HE HAD BEEN VERY MOODY LATELY ... BUT NOBODY SUSPECTED HE'D TAKE HIS OWN LIFE!"

"HE DIDN'T."

WHY DID THE CHIEF OF POLICE SAY IT WASN'T A SUICIDE?

IF BARTON DID NOT KILL HIMSELF, WHO MIGHT THE MURDERER BE? CONSIDER THESE CLUES: THE WOUND ON THE HEAD, THE POSITION OF THE BODY ON THE BENCH, THE GUN IN HIS HAND, AND THE MOTIVE.

THE CHIEF KNEW THAT IT WASN'T A SUICIDE. WILLIAM BARTON WAS KILLED BY SOMEONE ELSE IN ANOTHER PLACE!

wrap up

1. Imagine you are the police chief. Use evidence and clues from the conversations and the pictures to write a short report on the murder of William Barton.

2. If William Barton didn't commit suicide, who might his murderer be? Work in small groups to investigate the case. Search for new information, clues, evidence, and motives.

3. Brainstorm questions and answers for interviews with Mrs. Barton, William Barton's business parner, and a party guest. Then take turns to role-play each interview.

MYSTERY

:: That's some screen saver.

You Have Mail

Excerpt from *You Have Ghost Mail*
By Terence Blacker

warm up

In this story, the main character has a very scary experience. Share your own scary experiences with your class.

ADDRESS: www.youhaveghostmail.com

It was dark outside, and very still. In the walnut tree near the house of Matthew Bourne, a tawny owl shrieked, its harsh hunting cry cutting the night air before silence descended once more. The house itself slumbered, making only the sounds that a slumbering house would make. A fridge shuddered into life. A grandfather clock ticked. The sudden urgent scrabbling behind a wall betrayed the presence of a mouse.

Upstairs, in the bedroom of Matthew Bourne, something stirred. He had always been a good sleeper. So tonight Matthew had no idea that, within his room, not far from where he slept, other less familiar night noises could be heard. A click. An uncertain crackle. The sounds of electricity coming to life.

CHECKPOINT

Scan the first section of the story and write down all the words that have to do with sounds. Do you think if you read these words to someone that he or she would be able to guess what kind of story they were from?

Across the room, the screen of Matthew's new computer began to glow in the darkness. The light it shed was unlike that of normal computers. It was blood-red. After a few seconds, a small dark smudge appeared at the bottom of the screen. It rose, slowly and silently, like a bubble. When it reached the centre of the screen, it stayed uncertainly, swaying slightly. Seconds later, another dark mark appeared. It also moved slowly upwards and settled at the centre of the screen. Then another, and another.

---

slumbered: *slept*
shuddered: *shook from cold*

The four shapes hung there for several seconds. Then they began to become sharper and more focused until, unmistakably, they spelled out a single word.

HELP

After an hour, the image began to fade — first the letters, then the background, until only a small stain of red remained at the centre of the screen. Then that too disappeared and the computer was once more dark, silent, and untroubled. Outside, a rabbit screamed as a fox *pounced*, its sharp and deadly teeth closing on its victim's neck. And Matthew Bourne slept on.

• • • • • • • • • • • • •

Matthew knew a bit about computers. So when he was given an Epsilon 460 one Saturday late in October on his tenth birthday, he was able to set it up and get it going that evening without any problems.

It was Sunday morning that things started going wrong. The computer had seemed to be working more slowly than yesterday, as if it were having difficulty waking up. Then, just after he had started an email to his friend Angie, something strange happened. At that point, the screen froze. Matthew tapped several times on the keyboard. At first nothing happened. Then the letters of his email seemed to tremble and to vibrate, almost as if there were something behind them, within the computer, that was pushing to get through. As Matthew stared at the screen, a tiny dot became visible, pulsing and slowly growing larger. It was a single word.

HELP

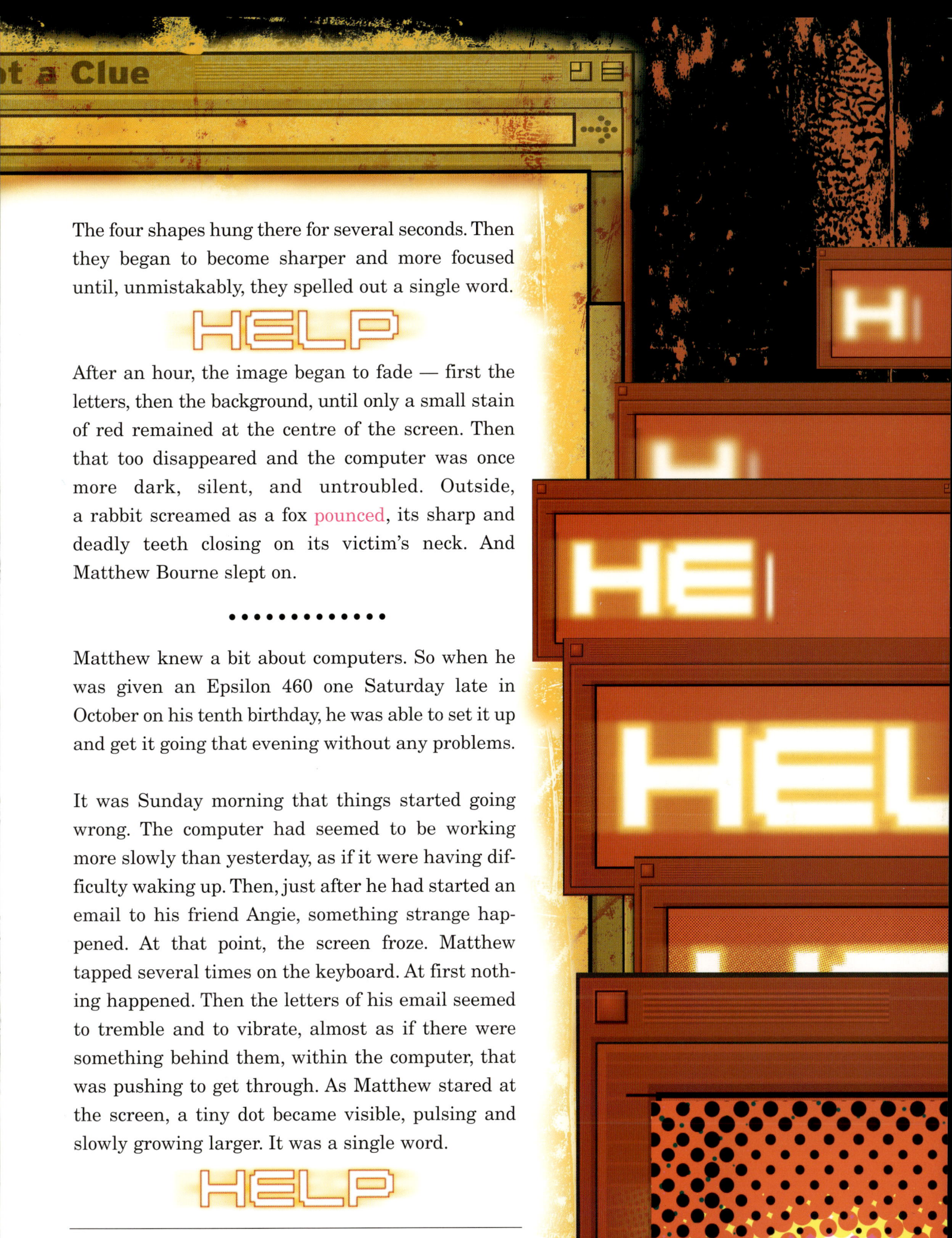

pounced: *jumped suddenly on something*

ADDRESS: www.youhaveghostmail.com

Matthew tapped once more. Nothing. He attempted to delete the email. But it was as if the computer had taken on a life of its own. Matthew stood up. He backed away from the computer, out of the room and down the corridor.

Maybe it was because he had been unable to eat much at dinner. Perhaps the weirdness with his computer was to blame. Whatever the reason, Matthew Bourne found it difficult to sleep that night.

But at some point in the night, he must have dozed off because suddenly Matthew found himself awakened with a start. The room was much colder now and there was an odd, musty smell of dampness in the air. Someone must have opened the door because, although Matthew was facing the wall, there was light in the room. He looked towards the door. It was closed. Slowly, Matthew turned, knowing in his heart what he would see. Across the room gazing at him, as if it were an eye in the night, was the computer. It glowed green, and the screen looked as if it were filled with water. His mouth dry, Matthew pushed back the duvet. He stood for a moment before his bed, a pale, illuminated figure. Then he moved toward the computer, forcing himself forward to the light. He looked deep into the image and saw, for the first time, a darkness — a sort of shadow — in the centre of the screen.

illuminated: *lit up*

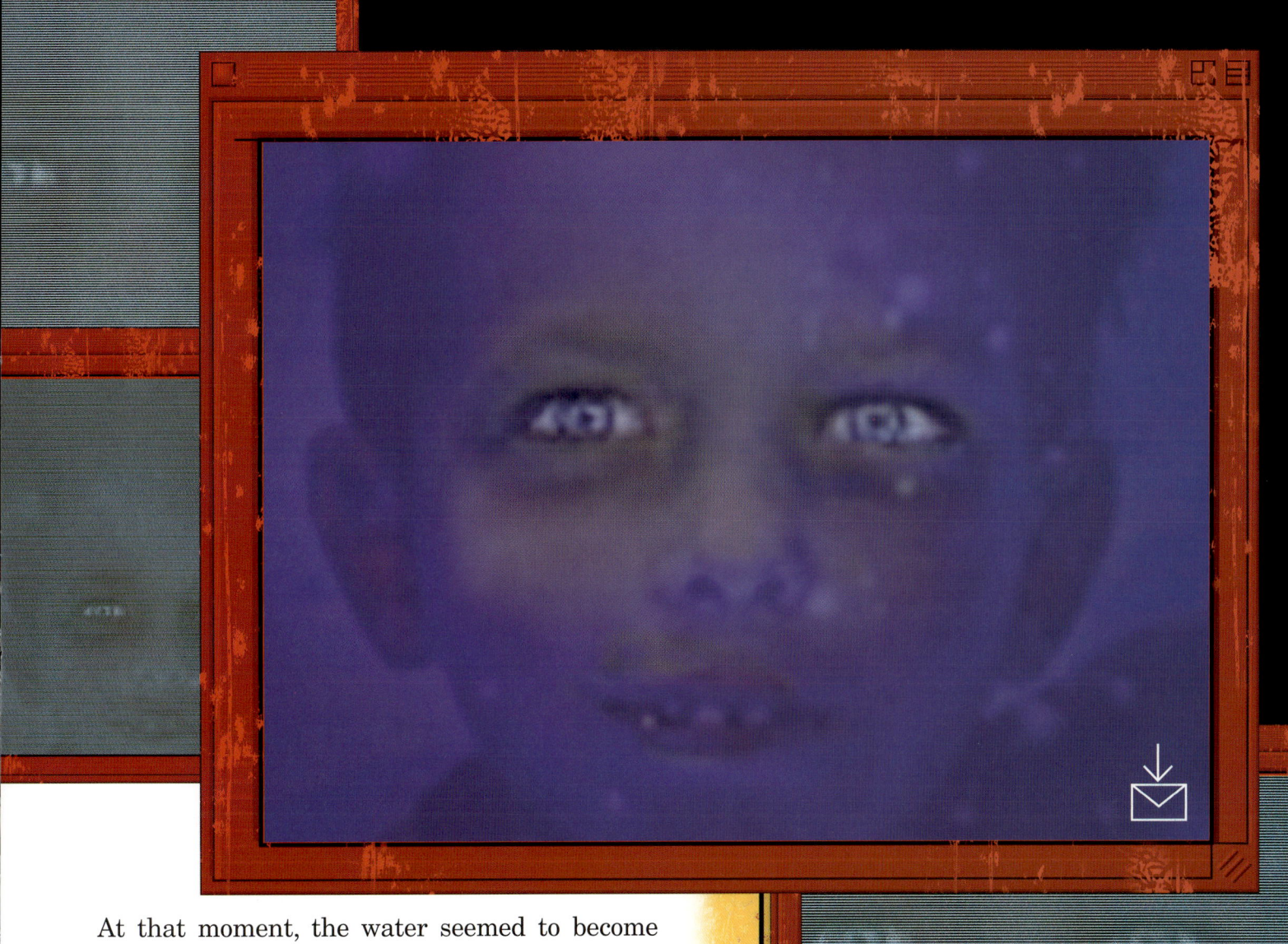

At that moment, the water seemed to become clearer and Matthew saw, as if it were daytime, as if it were real, what lay beneath the glittering surface. It was the face of a human, a boy. His eyes were wide, his mouth moving soundlessly. The dark hair on the boy's head moved backwards and forwards like dark seaweed caressed by the tide.

Matthew sat down slowly on the stool, gazing deep into the screen. The boy was quite young — maybe eight or nine years old. He seemed to be saying something, again and again, almost pleadingly. Instinctively, Matthew's fingers touched the keyboard. He tapped out the letters:

What do you want?

---

instinctively: *done without thinking*

Haven't Got a Clue

ADDRESS: www.youhaveghostmail.com

And a sound, a whisper, reached him, coming not from the computer but from the cold air around him.

"Don't … be … afraid … "

Matthew gazed deep into the screen. He typed:

Who are you?

"Child."

What kind of child?

"Not child." The voice was clipped and precise, strangely old-fashioned. "Giles. Giles Casson."

Giles?

"Help … me."

The room was filled with the sound of breathing — quick, uneven — like that of someone whose life was ebbing away. Matthew's hands, clammy with fear, hesitated over the keyboard. He tapped in a single word.

---

ebbing: *flowing, going*

How?

"Shall we be friends?"

The voice around him was faint, but almost playful.

Matthew noticed that the image on the screen seemed to be growing milky and indistinct, as if its energy was fading.

"Shall we be…" It was a whisper now, the sound of the wind in the walnut tree outside "… friends?"

The screen was dark, the room silent except for the sound of Matthew's own breathing. As if in a dream, he felt his way back to bed. He lay, staring upwards, the sound of his heart beating in his ears. Like a distant echo, within his mind or maybe outside it, the boy's voice was there, again and again.

"Shall we be friends?"

"Shall we be friends?"

"Shall we be friend

FYI

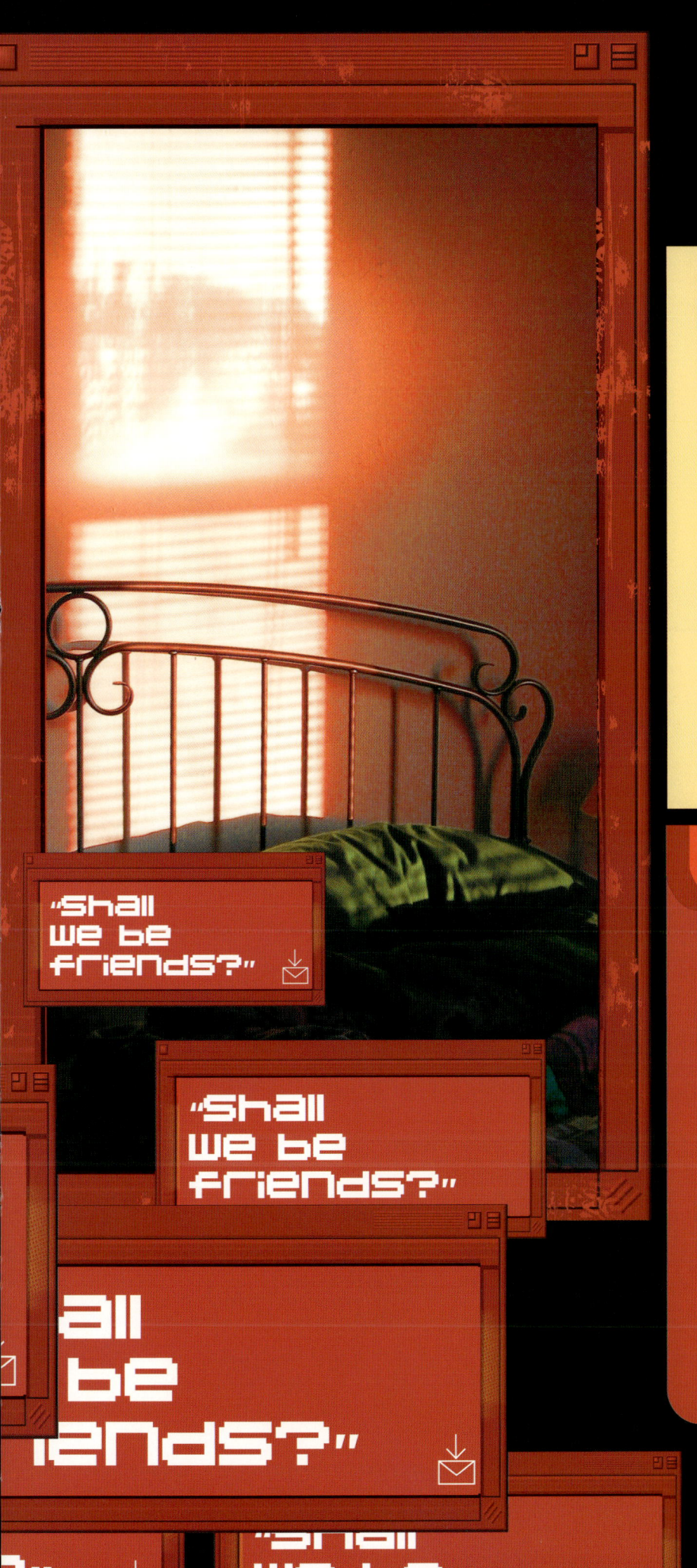

Although this story is fiction, there have been real reports of computers that are supposedly haunted. There was one in England in 1988 about a computer that was returned to a store because the customer said it kept turning itself on. The store technician couldn't find anything wrong with it. But the next morning when the storeowner came in, he found the computer switched on. At first, he thought that the technician had left it on. But when he went to turn the computer off, he discovered that it was unplugged!

wrap up

1. It takes the ghost three tries before it actually makes contact with Matthew. With a partner, make a list of the things that show something strange is going on in the story.

2. Reread the part in the last section of the story that describes what Matthew saw when he looked into his computer. Describe Matthew's feelings.

3. Write a short email from the boy to explain why he was trying to reach Matthew.

"Shall we be friends?"

"Shall we be friends?"

"Shall we be friends?"

"Shall we be friends?"

45

THE TERRIBLE

warm up

Think of other words that would mean the same as "terrible" for this poem. Consider why someone might walk on this path.

PATH
By Brian Patten

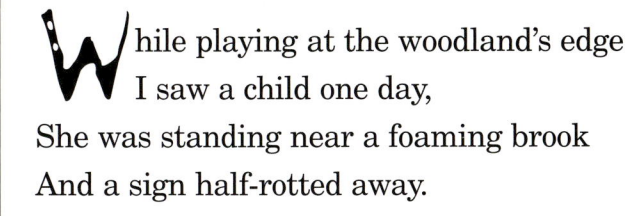

While playing at the woodland's edge
I saw a child one day,
She was standing near a foaming brook
And a sign half-rotted away.

There was something strange about her clothes;
They were from another age,
I might have seen them in a book
Upon a mildewed page.

She looked pale and frightened,
Her voice was thick with dread,
She spoke through lips rimmed with green
And this is what she said:

"I saw a signpost with no name,
I was surprised and had to stare,
It pointed to a broken gate
And a path that led nowhere.

"The path had run to seed and I
Walked as in a dream,
It entered a silent oak wood,
And crossed a silent stream.

"And in a tree a silent bird
Mouthed a silent song.
I wanted to turn back again
But something had gone wrong.

"The path would not let me go;
It had claimed me for its own,
It led me through a dark wood
Where all was overgrown.

"I followed it until the leaves
Had fallen from the trees,
I followed it until the frost
Drugged the autumn's bees.

"I followed it until the spring
Dissolved the winter snow,
And whichever way it turned
I was obliged to go.

"The years passed like shooting stars,
They melted and were gone,
But the path itself seemed endless,
It twisted and went on.

"I followed it and thought aloud,
'I'll be found, wait and see.'
Yet in my heart I knew by then
The world had forgotten me."

Frightened I turned homeward,
But stopped and had to stare.
I too saw that signpost with no name,
And the path that led nowhere.

wrap up

1. The poet has used words to create visual images. Prepare a list of words from the poem that paint a picture for you.

2. At the end of the poem, the narrator was caught in the terrible path. With a friend, discuss ideas and write one more verse for this poem. Your writing should explain what happened next.

mystery quiz answers

1. (d) Carolyn Keene is the author of the first 23 Nancy Drew mysteries.

2. (b) The Hardy boys are brothers. These two young detectives, Frank and Joe, have solved over 50 mysteries in this series written by Franklin W. Dixon.

3. (c) James Bond is a fictional character. The author of the James Bond spy books is Ian Fleming.

4. (d) Harry Potter is not a detective. He's a wizard.

5. (a) Inspector Gadget can be seen on cartoon shows. He uses very strange and clever inventions to help him solve crimes.

6. (d) The Bermuda Triangle is a mysterious place in the Atlantic Ocean. Many boats, planes, and people are believed to have disappeared in this area.

7. (d) Madonna was cast in this 1990 movie directed by Warren Beatty.

8. (c) A polygraph is a piece of equipment that is used by police. It helps them to decide if people are telling the truth by checking the rate of their pulse and breathing.

9. (b) The first three words in the call-up alphabet are Alpha Bravo Charlie. Police use this system of words rather than letters when identifying names and licence numbers; for example, Main St. would be Mike Alpha India November.

10. (a) Dr. Watson is Sherlock Holmes' friend. He helps Holmes solve mysteries by offering a listening ear and advice.

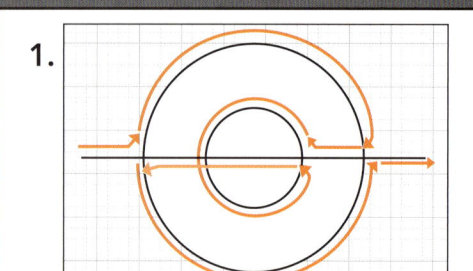

brain teaser answers

1.

2. Answer: It will take two minutes. It takes one minute for the front of the train to go over the bridge. It takes another minute for the back of the train to go over the bridge.

3. Answer: Jack

4. Answer: Friday.

5. Answer: There are six candies in the dish. Two are red, two are orange, and two are yellow.

6. Answer: There is no missing dollar. The $27 spent by the men is made up of the $25 charged for the room and the $2 kept by the bellboy. There is no reason to add $27 spent by the men and the $2 kept by the bellboy.

7. Answer: Friday was a horse.

8. Answer: The woman had triplets.

9. Answer: He was playing baseball, and the masked man was the catcher.

10. Answer: The doctor is her mother.